Contents

Introduction

'WE HAD A TERRIBLE WIND ALL DAY LONG,' SAID FIREFIGHTER MATT TIMMEL OF NEWBURGH, INDIANA, USA. 'IT JUST STARTED INCREASING AND INCREASING.'

That 'terrible wind' grew into a tornado – a swirling cone of wind and dust that swept across Kentucky and southern Indiana, in the USA, on 6 November 2005. The tornado did the most damage in Indiana, where it struck at about 2 am. Its raging winds caught most people asleep and off guard. Paul Adams remembered that he was sleeping when 'all of a sudden . . . the whole building shook, our window broke and there was water pouring in.' Paul's room-mate Tyler Moss said that 'it sounded like there was a jet engine in our apartment.'

Tornadoes, which are also called twisters, sweep up all sorts of material, called debris. That debris can include everything from stones and glass to lorries and livestock. When the storm had passed, it left behind splintered trees, wrecked homes and smashed cars. Chad Bennett, a Newburgh firefighter, described 'a whole apartment complex that lost all of the top floors of the units.' Newburgh resident Sherri Hudson saw her whole house ripped apart. She and her husband were lucky enough to reach their cellar safely, but, she said, 'we no sooner got down there than it was like a bomb exploded. All the debris came falling down the stair,' she said in an interview. 'The only thing left are the cabinets in my kitchen. The dishes are still in them untouched.'

A caravan frame was stuck atop a tree trunk after a tornado tore through Alberta, Canada, in July 2000.

The storm killed 24 people, injured at least 200 more and destroyed more than 500 homes. It was Indiana's deadliest tornado in more than 30 years.

TORNADOES

MICHAEL WOODS AND MARY B WOODS

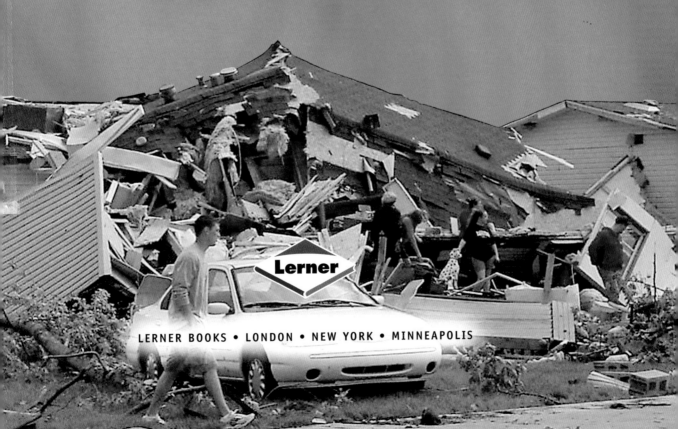

LERNER BOOKS • LONDON • NEW YORK • MINNEAPOLIS

To Dominic Calarco and Mary Vizzeri, Joseph Gullo and Martha Patti, Edward Boulle and Margaret Marshall, James Boyle and Catherine Golden

Editor's note: Determining the exact death toll following disasters is often difficult – if not impossible – especially in the case of disasters that took place long ago. The authors and the editors in this series have used their best judgement in determining which figures to include.

First published in the United Kingdom in 2008 by
Lerner Books,
Dalton House,
60 Windsor Avenue,
London SW19 2RR

Website address: www.lernerbooks.co.uk

This edition was updated and edited for UK publication by Discovery Books Ltd.,
Unit 3, 37 Watling Street, Leintwardine, Shropshire SY7 0LW

British Library Cataloguing in Publication Data

Woods, Michael, 1943-
    Tornadoes. - (Disasters up close)
    1. Tornadoes - Juvenile literature 2. Wind
damage -
    Juvenile literature
    I. Title II. Woods, Mary B.
    363.3'4923

ISBN-13: 978 1 58013 456 9

Printed in China

AWESOME DISASTERS

Tornadoes are some of nature's most amazing and powerful storms. Winds rush as fast as 480 kilometres per hour (480 kmph). Twisters arrive with a roar that many people compare to the sound of a freight train. The strongest storms can lift train carriages weighing more than 45 tonnes and throw them onto their sides.

More than a thousand tornadoes strike every year. Most of them are in the United States of America. However, tornadoes are common in other parts of the world, too. Australia, New Zealand, South America and parts of Asia and Europe often experience tornadoes, although only occasionally are they bad enough to kill people. Britain has more tornadoes than almost any other country in Europe. Usually these tornadoes are very weak and do little damage. In the United States, however, they can be very fierce and every year people are killed.

Residents of Evansville, Indiana, USA, clean up after the powerful November 2005 twister tore apart their home.

'When I woke up, [it] sounded like hail hitting the window and all of a sudden the whole house just exploded.'

– Casey Lockhart, describing the November 2005 tornado that hit his rural Indiana home

Terrible Tornadoes

TORNADOES ARE AMONG THE WORLD'S SMALLEST YET MOST VIOLENT STORMS. THEY ARE FUNNEL-SHAPED AREAS OF AIR THAT SPIN VERY FAST. WINDS IN SOME TORNADOES SWIRL AT MORE THAN 480 KMPH. THAT'S FOUR TIMES FASTER THAN A CAR DRIVES ON THE MOTORWAY.

People sometimes call tornadoes twisters. These spiral-shaped clouds do twist through the air. Twisters form in certain kinds of thunderstorms. In fact, the word *tornado* comes from the Spanish word *tronada*, which means 'thunderstorm'.

'It looked like a big cloud of wind coming,' said Shirley Reale, a retired school secretary. 'Stuff was flying everywhere.' In 2004 a twister hit her home in Campbelltown, Pennsylvania, USA

WHIRLING WINDS

Tornadoes don't always hit the ground. Sometimes they blow along many metres above the land. If a tornado does touch the ground, the spinning wind can cause great damage. Tornadoes don't stay in one place. They move across the ground, damaging everything in their path. A tornado may stay on the ground for seconds or hours.

A tornado's winds push and tear at buildings and other structures. Powerful twisters can rip apart houses, schools and shops. They can tear down trees, electric power lines and telephone lines. The wind scatters heavy objects almost like a fan blowing a stack of paper across a tabletop.

MINI-CYCLONES

Tornadoes are the smallest kind of cyclones; storms with wind that spins in a circle. Most twisters are about as wide as several football pitches end to end. Hurricanes and typhoons are the biggest cyclones. Some of them can get as wide as a small country.

A tornado in Aken, Germany, in June 2004. The tornado partially destroyed nearly 100 buildings in the small town.

Strong tornadoes can't carry people to other worlds, as the tornado in the film *The Wizard of Oz* did to Dorothy. They can pick up people, cows, cars, vans and even mobile homes. The whirling wind can make these objects sail through the air and fall down far away. One tornado picked up a motel sign in Broken Bow, Oklahoma, USA, and dropped it 50 km (30 miles) away in another state.

The famous tornado scene from the 1939 film *The Wizard of Oz* carries Dorothy's house *(below)* to Oz.

D IS FOR DAMAGE

Wind causes most tornado damage. Lightning and hail from thunderstorms that form tornadoes can add to the damage. The severe thunderstorms that come before tornadoes may produce hail the size of golf balls. This hail can smash windows, dent the metal on cars and destroy farmers' crops.

Don E Halsey took pictures of the damage in Xenia, Ohio, USA, after a tornado struck in 1974. 'The picture that amazed me the most was of an automobile rolled up into a near perfect ball,' he said. Someone had driven the car right into the tornado.

SUCKED UP

Dorothy and her little dog, Toto, got sucked up into a tornado in *The Wonderful Wizard of Oz*, a book by L Frank Baum. In real life, many things do get caught in tornadoes – including people, sometimes. But tornadoes don't usually hurt people by lifting them high into the sky. Instead, most tornado injuries and deaths occur when people are thrown to the side by wind or are hit by debris.

A 1950 Texas tornado carried this house 25 metres before setting it down on its side.

Two residents of Brandenburg, Kentucky, USA, pick through debris after the 1974 tornado destroyed half the town.

'The next thing I saw was a scene I shall never forget.... destruction you read about that happens to other places, but never to your own.'

– John J Scott, describing Brandenburg, Kentucky, after a 1974 tornado

When tornadoes hit towns and cities they can cause terrible disasters because many people and buildings are close together. These whirlwinds cause billions of dollars of damage in the United States each year. Tornadoes kill about 70 people every year and seriously injure about 1,500 others.

In early May 2003, tornadoes caused more than 40 deaths during a single week. Almost four hundred tornadoes broke out in Oklahoma and more than a dozen other US states during that week. That's more than in any other week in US history.

David Waller had a close shave with one of those twisters. He was driving an eighteen-wheel tractor-trailer lorry on a motorway near Oklahoma City, Oklahoma, on 8 May 2003. Suddenly, in the distance, he saw a tornado coming right towards him. Waller pulled to the side of the road and jumped into a ditch to take shelter. Then the fierce storm picked up his truck and dropped it on one side. He later remembered being 'scared to death'.

Several days earlier, weather forecasters had seen that conditions were perfect for a tornado outbreak. They issued warnings as twisters approached. These warnings gave many people time to take shelter from the twisters, but they could not save everyone or everything. In that one terrible week, hundreds of people were injured and thousands of homes and businesses were badly damaged. The cost of the destruction totalled hundreds of millions of dollars.

THE GREAT NATCHEZ TORNADO

One of the worst tornadoes in history hit the Mississippi town of Natchez on 7 May 1840. History books say that it killed 317 people. However, the real number of deaths may have been much higher. At that time, people in the southern United States owned slaves. Officials didn't bother to count slaves who died on plantations (large farms) because slaves were considered property. We may never know how many slaves died in the Great Natchez Tornado.

A twister approaches a house in Kansas, USA, in 2004. The US National Weather Service recorded 1,717 tornados in the United States that year, an all-time record.

1880 MARSHFIELD TORNADO

A damaged street in Marshfield, Missouri.

An eight-year-old boy named W D Chitty was the weather forecaster for the great Marshfield, Missouri, tornado, in the USA. On 18 April 1880, Chitty looked out the window. He saw what looked like a cone-shaped column of smoke billowing into the air near a neighbour's house.

'I grabbed my father's knee and said, 'Look. Cohen's house is on fire.' . . . My father looked steadily for a moment and then leaped to his feet with a cry, 'My God, it's a tornado!' Chitty and his family ran to take shelter in the town courthouse, one of the sturdiest buildings in town. *'The square was filled with excited people running in all directions and looking and pointing at the approaching funnel-like cloud,'* he remembered. *'The wind had

12

Dust and debris hang in the air over the ruins of Marshfield. }

‘ *The wind . . . rose to a fiendish shriek.* ’

– W D Chitty

risen so rapidly that in the few seconds it took to get across the courthouse yard, my father had to pull my mother by main strength to get her into the lobby.'

After the wind stopped, nobody dared to leave the shelter for a few minutes. When they did, people saw a wrecked town. The Chittys' house was in a block of strong brick buildings. The tornado, however, easily ripped off the second storey of the buildings. *'We instinctively moved towards the direction of what had been our home, but what was now nothing but a barren floor with a few remnants of shattered walls and rubbish,'* Chitty said.

This massive twister was one of the 25 most deadly tornado disasters in US history. It killed about 90 people and injured about 200 others. The tornado damaged nearly every building in town. Chitty's family and dozens of others lost their homes.

Musician John W Boone honoured the Marshfield disaster and its victims in song. His piano tune 'Marshfield Tornado' sounded like the roar of a tornado. The twister tune, however, was disastrous for the piano. When Boone tried to record it, he played so loudly and the song had so many notes that the piano broke.

What Causes Tornadoes?

PEOPLE IN KANSAS, MISSOURI AND SIX OTHER US STATES WERE ENJOYING A PLEASANT SPRING DAY ON 4 MAY, 2003. BUT TWO AIR MASSES WERE ABOUT TO SEND THEM RUNNING FOR SHELTER. AN AIR MASS IS A LARGE BODY OF AIR. DIFFERENT AIR MASSES HAVE DIFFERENT TEMPERATURES AND MOISTURE LEVELS. THEY CAN BE WARM OR COLD AND DRY OR MOIST. WHEN THEY MEET, TORNADOES FORM.

One mass of cold, dry air moved southwards from the Rocky Mountains. Another mass of warm, moist air came northwards from the Gulf of Mexico. When the two air masses mixed together, 94 tornadoes formed in eight US states. The twisters killed 38 people and caused around $150 million worth of damage.

'The atmosphere created a perfect set up for a . . . spring severe weather outbreak,' said Dan McCarthy, a meteorologist. Meteorologists report and forecast the weather. They also study conditions in the atmosphere that cause storms and other kinds of weather. The atmosphere is the layer of air above the Earth's surface.

THE NO-NO WORD

Until 1952 weather forecasters in the United States could not use the word *tornado* in forecasts. Government officials banned the word because tornado forecasts were not reliable. They worried that a prediction could do even more harm than a tornado. It might make people panic. They could get hurt trying to escape. The ban ended after tornado forecasting improved in the late 1940s.

Kansas meteorology students monitor a storm for tornado-related activity.

Trees were broken in half by a
tornado that swept through
China in June 2005.

INGREDIENTS IN THE RECIPE

Most tornadoes form in severe thunderstorms called supercells. Not all bad thunderstorms produce tornadoes. Meteorologists don't know exactly why some thunderstorms produce deadly twisters and others don't. They have, however, learned a lot about supercells.

For supercells to form, the atmosphere must have certain ingredients. First, the air must have enough moisture to feed the storm. That moisture comes from water vapour, which is liquid water that has evaporated and changed into an invisible gas. Water vapour makes the air feel humid. Tornadoes also need a layer of warm air near the ground, with a layer of cold air above it.

These conditions occur when cold air masses plough into warm masses of air. As the different air masses meet, they form a boundary called a weather front. Along the front, the warm, moist air rises in currents called updraughts. The warm air grows cooler as it rises. As it cools, the water vapour in the air condenses, or changes back to a liquid. Those tiny drops of water form towering thunderclouds.

An anvil cloud (a flat-topped cloud that makes up part of a thunderstorm) at sunset.

The change from a gas to a liquid releases heat. Heat helps the air to continue rising, until it reaches heights of 9,000 m or more. At about that level, the air stops rising. It spreads sideways to form a flat-topped thunderstorm cloud.

This high school in Monticello, Indiana, USA, was flattened by a killer tornado in 1974.

PUTTING THE TWIST IN TWISTERS

The next step in making a twister is for the rising air to start spinning. Something called wind shear makes this happen. Wind shear occurs when winds at different heights move in different directions, different speeds or both. Wind shear produces a wide, horizontal tube of rapidly spinning air.

Sometimes, as updraughtss continue rising and downdraughts blow towards the Earth, they push on the spinning tube of air until it stands on end. This upright column of wind is called a mesocyclone. The mesocyclone is the part of the storm that actually produces tornadoes. It spins faster and faster through the supercell. Nearby clouds spin along with it, sometimes dropping a little lower in a huge wall cloud. This massive cloud formation looks like a dark wall of clouds hanging in the sky. Sometimes the wall cloud itself will spin for thirty minutes or so and then disappear. At other times, it will produce a tornado that drops down out of the cloud.

A mesocyclone and wall cloud may form one tornado or several at the same time. However, only about half of mesocyclones produce tornadoes. Some mesocyclones run out of the warm, moist air that releases heat and keeps updraughts going. They dry up and fizzle out.

A TWISTER IN YOUR SINK

Fill up a sink, and watch water run down the drain *(above)*. You'll see a little whirlpool that forms at the plughole. This whirlpool is called a vortex. A vortex is water or air that spins. A tornado is a vortex of air.

A mesocyclone created this tornado, which struck Oklahoma, USA, in May 1999.

TWISTER TOTALS

Millions of thunderstorms occur each year. Fortunately, only rare storms produce tornadoes. In an average year, 800 to 1,200 tornadoes are reported in the United States. More twisters probably strike in remote areas where nobody notices or reports them.

FUN FACT

A tornado's strong winds can carry small objects for great distances. In 1915 a bank cheque may have taken the longest journey. The Great Bend Tornado carried the cheque more than 300 km (200 miles), taking it from Kansas to the neighbouring state of Nebraska.

In Britain tornadoes usually do little damage, but in 2005 a tornado hit Birmingham injuring twenty people and causing damage to about a 100 homes. A year later a tornado hit part of London with wind speeds of over 130 kmph. It damaged over 150 houses and many cars. The estimated cost of repairs ran into the millions. Luckily only a small number of people were injured.

A damaged shop in Birmingham, England, after a tornado struck the city on 28 July 2005. Trees were uprooted and roofs ripped off houses. Cars were thrown about

THE FORMATION OF A TORNADO

A warm, moist air front meets a cold, dry front.

A weather front forms. Updraughts create thunderclouds.

A supercell forms.

Wind shear creates a spinning tube of air.

Updraughts and downdraughtss create a mesocyclone. A wall cloud drops down.

A tornado forms and touches down.

1925 TRI-STATE TORNADO

A group of men survey the damage in Griffin, Indiana, USA.

Weather experts predicted strong shifting winds for eastern Missouri, southern Illinois, and south-western Indiana for 18 March 1925. Nobody dreamed how forcefully the wind would actually blow.

At 1.01 pm, a tornado hit in Ellington, Missouri. Trees began to snap like toothpicks. Within three and a half hours, this twister would become the deadliest in US history. People called it the Tri-State Tornado because it travelled 350 km (220 miles) through three states – Missouri, Illinois and Indiana.

'Boards, poles, cans, garments, stoves, whole sides of the little frame houses, in some cases the houses themselves, were picked up and smashed to earth,' a newspaper reporter wrote about the storm. 'And living beings, too. A baby was blown from its mother's arms. A cow, picked up by the wind, was hurled into the village restaurant.'

Lela Hartman was only four years

old when the tornado struck. Lela was visiting her grandmother's farm near West Frankfort, Illinois. **'It just kept getting darker and darker,'** she remembered many years later. **'It was almost as black as night when we finally went to the cellar.'** The family was safe in their underground storm cellar, but when they came out, Lela noticed that the storm had done something odd to her grandma's house.

'It . . . turned the house on the foundation,' Lela remembered. **'That was a big, big ol' house, and it turned it on the foundation.'** The twister lifted the entire house and swung it around so that the front door faced in a different direction.

The air was filled with 10,000 things.

– a reporter for the Saint Louis Post-Dispatch newspaper

Everyone agreed that the Tri-State Tornado was huge. **'It was so wide,'** said Eugene Porter, who lived in Murphysboro, Illinois. F M Hewitt, in De Soto, Illinois, described a **'seething, boiling mass of clouds. . . . [and] a roaring noise as of many trains.'**

One young girl in Gorham, Illinois, remembered the twister hitting the town's school. **'I can't describe it,'** she said. **'I can't bear to think about it. Children all around me were cut and bleeding. They cried and screamed. It was something awful. I had to close my eyes.'**

In all, the Tri-State Tornado killed almost 700 people and injured about 2,000 others. Many thousands lost their homes. The twister destroyed or severely damaged ten towns, including homes, schools and other buildings.

A school in De Soto, Illinois, lay in ruins after the massive 1925 tornado swept through.

Tornado Alley

TORNADOES CAN OCCUR IN MANY PLACES AROUND THE WORLD. THE UNITED STATES HAS FAR MORE TORNADOES THAN ANY OTHER COUNTRY. IN FACT, ABOUT THREE-QUARTERS OF ALL TORNADOES IN THE WORLD HIT THE UNITED STATES. TWISTERS CAN HAPPEN ALL OVER THE COUNTRY. HOWEVER, THEY ARE MOST COMMON IN THE MID-WEST, SOUTH-EAST AND SOUTH-WEST OF THE COUNTRY.

One area gets so many tornadoes that people call it Tornado Alley. It is located in the centre of the United States (see map on page 27). The weather in Tornado Alley is often perfect for the formation of tornadoes. Warm, moist air masses flow into the area from the Gulf of Mexico. They meet colder, drier air that often flows in from the west and north. When these air masses collide, thunderstorms and tornadoes can result.

Tornadoes rarely hit large cities, but that does not make them safe from a storm. This tornado formed over central Dallas, Texas, in April 1960.

Tornadoes have tremendous power. They have been known to drive many objects through trees, like this record (left).

24

ANYTIME STORMS

Tornadoes can strike at any time of the year, but most twisters happen during tornado season, which, in the US lasts from March to August. The most dangerous months of all are March, April and May. During that time, the Tornado Alley area is still cool and dry from winter. When wet, warm air flows in from the Gulf of Mexico, storms start to form.

By summertime, the air in most of Tornado Alley has become warmer. It is closer in temperature to the Gulf of Mexico's air masses. As a result, the number of tornadoes decreases. Tornadoes, however, can form during hurricanes, which continue to occur until late autumn. In September 2004, Hurricane Ivan produced almost 100 tornadoes.

Tornadoes can also happen at any time of the day. Just like thunderstorms, however, tornadoes are most common in the afternoon and evening. By then the sun has heated up the air. The warm air rises in the updraughts that help form thunderclouds – and sometimes tornadoes.

DID YOU KNOW?

Waterspouts *(above)* are tornadoes that occur over water. They can damage boats, docks and other structures. Some are tornadoes that formed from storms over land and travelled over a lake or other body of water. Others form over the water in fair weather and cause less damage.

DISASTER ZONES

About 75 per cent of the world's tornadoes strike in North America's Tornado Alley (shown in red). This map shows where some notable twisters have struck.

ASIA

Hamburg, Germany
Birmingham, England

EUROPE

Dakha, Bangladesh
1969 (540 deaths)

Jessore, Bangladesh
near Ludhiana, India

AFRICA

Central Bangladesh
1996 (more than 600 deaths)

Calcutta, India

New Delhi, India
1978 (28 deaths)

Mount Ayliff, South
Africa 1999 (25 deaths)

AUSTRALIA

Sydney,
Australia 2001

New Richmond, Wisconsin
1889 (119 deaths)

NORTH AMERICA

Flint, Michigan

Xenia, Ohio
Worcester, Massachusetts

Omaha, Nebraska
1975 (more than 4000 buildings damaged)

Tri-State Tornado
1925 (nearly 700 deaths)

Limon, Colorado

St. Louis, Missouri

Western Tenessee

Gainesville, Georgia

Oklahoma Tornado Outbreak
1999 (41 deaths)

Natchez, Mississippi

Marshfield Missouri

Pampa, Texas

Wichita Falls, Texas
1979 (more than 40 deaths)

SOUTH AMERICA

San Justo,
Argentina 1973

A worker surveys the torn. damage to a couple's hom in Xenia, Ohio, USA.

1974
TORNADO
SUPER OUTBREAK

Eight-year-old Rick Hoag was watching television at home in Xenia, Ohio, USA, on 3 April 1974. His mum called from work to tell Rick and his dad that a bad storm was on the way. *'She told me to make sure the garage door was shut and stay inside,'* Rick recalled.

Soon the electricity went out. Rick looked out of the window. A whirling column of wind was heading right towards the house. It twisted and

turned like a giant snake. One end was high in the sky. The other end touched the ground, tearing apart everything in its path.

'I think back often to that day,' Rick said.

As the wind howled, Rick and his dad took shelter in a small bathroom. His dad sat on the floor with his back against the door, bracing his feet against the opposite wall. Then the storm hit, with a roar like a hundred trains. It began tearing the house apart. Windows broke, walls cracked and wind rushed up under the bathroom floor.

The massive 1974 tornado approaches Xenia, Ohio.

'I asked [Dad] if we were flying,' Rick remembered. 'When things calmed down we opened the door.' Rick and his father saw that much of their house was simply gone. 'The odd feeling I had,' Rick said, 'looking up the street from inside what once was my hallway, is still with me today.'

> ## The sound was tremendous.
>
> – Rick Hoag

The series of April tornadoes was the worst tornado outbreak in US history. Known as the Super Outbreak, it included 148 tornadoes. They hit in a 4,000-km (2,500-mile) path of destruction covering thirteen states and parts of Canada. At one point, fifteen twisters were on the ground at the same time.

Strong winds in the storms picked up cars and mobile homes and carried them away. Wind pulled trees out of the ground. The storms tore apart houses, shops, schools and other buildings.

All the broken pieces – sharp glass, splinters of wood, bricks and tree branches – whipped through the air at more than 160 kmph. The debris caused more damage when it hit people and buildings. In sixteen hours, the storms killed 350 people and injured more than 6,000. About 27,500 buildings were damaged. The cost of repairs was more than $600 million.

This house in Xenia was cut in half by the tornado that ripped through the town.

Measuring a Menace

WHEN PEOPLE HEAR ABOUT A TORNADO, THEY WONDER WHETHER IT WAS STRONG ENOUGH TO CAUSE A DISASTER. THEY ALSO WANT TO KNOW HOW ITS STRENGTH COMPARED TO TORNADOES IN THE PAST.

After a 1974 tornado in Brandenburg, Kentucky, USA, parents asked those questions as they drove towards the high school to find their children. 'All of us were yelling to each other in other cars, asking what had been hit, who had been hurt, where was the worst damage,' said Libby Brown. Her daughter was in the school. 'And nobody knew.'

In the past, people could only guess at how strong a tornado had been. Have you ever heard the expression, 'Appearances can be deceiving?' That's true for tornadoes. Big tornadoes can have weak winds and cause little damage. Small tornadoes can be very strong and cause great disasters.

DR TORNADO

In 1951 T Theodore Fujita invented a way to measure tornadoes. He was a famous weather scientist who knew so much about twisters that people called him Dr Tornado. The measuring system is usually called the Fujita scale. Sometimes it is also called the Fujita-Pearson tornado scale after Allen Pearson, another scientist who helped develop it.

Fujita realized that it would be difficult to make direct measurements of tornado winds. Tornadoes last only a short time. They occur without giving much advance warning.

BIGGEST TORNADO

The 1925 Tri-State Tornado in Missouri, Illinois and Indiana probably was the biggest tornado ever recorded. People said it was more than 1.6 km (1 mile) across. Modern scientists, however, are not sure whether it was one monster twister or a 'family' of many tornadoes that came from one storm.

This rubble marks all that is left of a house after a tornado touched down in Worcester, Massachusetts, USA, in June 1953.

In 1951, it was impossible to send measuring instruments to the places where tornadoes were happening.

Fujita decided to measure the strength of tornadoes by the amount of damage they caused. Fujita knew that only winds of certain strengths could tear roofs off houses, blow down brick walls and overturn trains. If a tornado caused such damage, its winds must have been of a certain strength.

INCREDIBLE, INCONCEIVABLE TORNADOES

The Fujita scale goes from F0 to F6. An F0 is the weakest tornado, with winds of 64 to 116 kmph. This type of twister is strong enough to damage chimneys, break branches off trees and push over trees with very shallow roots. An F3 tornado has winds of 254 to 332 kmph. These winds can overturn railway trains, tear roofs off houses and topple trees with deep roots.

An F5 on the Fujita scale is an 'incredible tornado'. With winds of 420 to 512 kmph, it can throw cars more than 100 m – further than the length of a football pitch.

Dr Tornado saved F6 for the 'inconceivable tornado'. With winds up to 610 kmph, it would destroy almost everything in its path. Such a tornado has never been recorded, but it is definitely possible.

The Fujita scale depends on the judgement of people who check the damage. It takes highly trained individuals to make a judgement. Different people may make different judgements. Since February 2007 a

Theodore Fujita works with a tornado simulator in 1979 in his lab at the University of Chicago.

FASTEST WINDS

The fastest winds ever measured in a tornado were 512 kmph. A car going that fast could travel 8 km (5 miles) in just one minute. Joshua Wurman, a tornado researcher at the University of Oklahoma, measured the wind speed during a 3 May 1999, twister near Oklahoma City.

THE ENHANCED FUJITA SCALE

SINCE 2007, SCIENTISTS HAVE BEEN USING AN UPDATED FUJITA SCALE WITH REDEFINED WIND SPEEDS. TORNADOES THAT HAPPENED IN THE PAST HAVE NOT BEEN RE-CATEGORIZED, BUT ALL FUTURE TORNADOES WILL BE RANKED ACCORDING TO THIS ENHANCED FUJITA SCALE.

CATEGORY	WIND SPEED	TYPE OF DAMAGE
EF0	105–137 KMPH	LIGHT DAMAGE. SOME DAMAGE TO CHIMNEYS; BRANCHES BROKEN OFF TREES; SHALLOW-ROOTED TREES PUSHED OVER.
EF1	138–177 KMPH	MOBILE HOMES OVERTURNED; MOVING CARS PUSHED OFF ROADS; ATTACHED GARAGES MAY BE DESTROYED.
EF2	179–217 KMPH	ROOFS TORN OFF SOME HOUSES; MOBILE HOMES DEMOLISHED; TRAIN CARRIAGES OVERTURNED; LARGE TREES UPROOTED.
EF3	219–266 KMPH	ROOFS AND SOME WALLS TORN OFF STRONG HOUSES; TRAINS OVERTURNED; MOST TREES UPROOTED; HEAVY CARS LIFTED OFF GROUND AND THROWN.
EF4	237–322 KMPH	STRONG HOUSES LEVELLED; WEAKER HOUSES BLOWN AWAY SOME DISTANCE; CARS THROWN.
EF5	MORE THAN 322 KMPH	STRONG HOUSES LIFTED OFF FOUNDATIONS AND CARRIED CONSIDERABLE DISTANCES; CARS THROWN MORE THAN 100 M; BARK TORN OFF TREES; INCREDIBLE THINGS WILL OCCUR.

A tornado forms near Red Rock, Oklahoma, USA, in May 2003.

revised version of the Fujita scale has been used to make it more accurate. Fortunately, about 74 per cent of all tornadoes are the relatively weak F0 or F1 storms. About 25 per cent are F2 or F3. Only 1 per cent are the very violent F4 and F5 storms. However, forecasters can't predict the strength of a tornado in advance. That makes it important for people to take each tornado seriously. It may be an F0 or an F5.

TORNADO TURTLES

One of the most important tools for measuring strong storms and tornadoes is Doppler radar. Radar uses invisible radio waves to locate objects. Doppler radar is a special kind of radar. It can show and measure wind directions and wind speeds. Doppler radar images can tell forecasters when a tornado is forming inside a mesocyclone.

Another tool is the anemometer, which measures wind speeds. This instrument has little cups that catch the wind. Then the cups spin around at speeds that show the strength of the wind.

An anemometer cannot take measurements inside a tornado. The strong winds would tear the instrument apart. So scientists sometimes use tools called turtles. These turtles are packages of instruments covered with armour, like an army tank. Scientists leave them in the storm's path, where they can get sucked right up into a twister without breaking. Turtles measure air pressure, temperature and moisture levels.

THE NOAA

The NOAA is the National Oceanic and Atmospheric Administration. It is part of the US government, and it includes the National Weather Service. The Weather Service forecasts weather conditions. NOAA also does scientific research on better ways to predict and respond to tornadoes and other severe weather.

This Doppler radar unit was the first one used by the United States Weather Bureau. The Bureau was an early form of the National Weather Service.

U.S. DEPT. OF COMMERCE
WEATHER BUREAU
EXPERIMENTAL TORNADO DETECTION RADA'.

‘ *There was nothing that was recognizable.* **Nothing!** ’

– Ron Wert, describing the destruction of an F5 tornado that hit western Michigan in 1956

The 1956 tornado that hit Michigan, USA, turned this field into a scrapyard. Homes smashed to pieces and vehicles turned on their sides were only part of the damage done by the violent storm.

1979 WICHITA FALLS TORNADO

The devastation in Wichita Falls, Texas, USA, following the 1979 F5 tornado was widespread.

On Tuesday 10 April the tornado sirens of Wichita Falls, Texas, USA sounded out a warning. People expected an ordinary twister. What they got was a monster tornado that measured 2.5 km (1.5 miles) across.

Wilma Rickard and a friend were at a shopping centre with their children when the tornado hit. She remembered that the wind *'blew and it blew and it blew. One second it felt like it was going to flatten you like a pancake. . . . And then, the next second, it felt like it was going to pick you up and throw you through the roof. And it would do that over and over and over.'*

'Then it stopped. We got up. I realized all the rain I thought was going to drown us was really debris

The massive Wichita Falls tornado stacked these cars on top of one another.

'I'll never forget it as long as I live.'

– Wilma Rickard

hitting us. . . . I then saw the wall in front of me. Most of it was gone. It had pipes with water spraying out everywhere. And you could smell gas. My friend was bloody, but the kids and I were fine.'

Other people were not so lucky. Some tried to escape the tornado in their cars. The wind blew cars off the road and stacked them up one on top of another in the shopping centre parking lot.

'The suffering and destruction caused by the Wichita Falls tornado is nearly inconceivable,' a National Weather Service meteorologist wrote in his report. *'The passage of a violent tornado through an 8-mile [13 km] section of a city is an almost*

The 1979 twister upended many heavy objects, such as cars, as if they weighed nothing.

unheard-of natural disaster.'

The twister was the worst of thirteen tornadoes that snaked through the Red River valley that day, hitting the states of Texas, Oklahoma and Arkansas. Advance warnings saved many people's lives, but in Wichita Falls alone, the tornado killed more than 40 people and injured about 1,800. The twister also destroyed or damaged more than 5,000 homes, causing damage estimated at $400 million. People still call that day Terrible Tuesday.

People Helping People

IN A DISASTER, PEOPLE FIRST FEEL SHOCK AND NUMBNESS. THEY MIGHT NOT EVEN BELIEVE THAT A TWISTER IS ROARING TOWARDS THEIR HOME OR SCHOOL. PEOPLE FEAR FOR THEIR OWN SAFETY AND FOR THEIR FAMILIES, FRIENDS AND PETS. THEY WANT TO FIND A SAFE PLACE TO TAKE SHELTER.

People who survive a disaster often need help to recover. Recovery means getting life back to normal again. Tornadoes and other disasters may kill or injure family members, friends and pets. Survivors feel grief for the injured and dead. Disasters can also destroy peoples' homes and everything that they owned.

'What we saw has never left me since,' remembered Lisa Irene Hale. She was just ten years old during the great 1974 tornado outbreak. Lisa and her mother took shelter in a greengrocers in Xenia, Ohio, USA. After the tornado passed, Lisa remembered, 'there were people walking in the street, but no one said a word. It was a deafening, numbing silence.'

Survivors of a tornado disaster need water, food, clothing and warm blankets. They may also need a place to live until new homes can be built. Wreckage must be cleared away so new buildings can be constructed. Workers must restore electricity and telephone service.

Shop owners in Pierce City, Missouri, USA, embrace after their businesses were damaged by a 2003 tornado.

A woman in Moore, Oklahoma, USA, takes a break from clearing up after a May 2003 tornado.

NEIGHBOURS HELPING NEIGHBOURS

Tornadoes usually affect only a small area. This makes it easier for help to arrive from outside the disaster area. But at first, people may have to help themselves and one another. This can be difficult right after disaster strikes. People affected by a twister are often in a state of shock.

'People were walking, dazed and hushed,' said Jim Brocker, who was in La Plata, Maryland, USA, minutes after a 2002 tornado. 'In the stillness, one woman ran screaming towards a damaged motel. People tried to stop her, ask her if she was OK, but she just kept running and screaming.'

Still, neighbours have always helped neighbours. 'My father left immediately to help in gathering up and caring for the wounded,' said W D Chitty, remembering the 1880 tornado in Marshfield, Missouri. The tornado destroyed the Chittys' house, but his family worked hard to help others after the twister.

DISASTER RELIEF WORKERS

Help from outside is also very important after a tornado strikes. In the United States assistance may come from disaster relief teams sent by the Federal Emergency Management Agency (FEMA), which is part of the US government. In big disasters the army would be called in. They can fly in huge loads of supplies and experienced aid workers. When a tornado or other disaster hits Britain it is usually the police, fire and ambulance services that arrive on the scene first. Other organizations like the Red Cross and the Salvation Army may provide more assistance if needed.

STORM SPOTTERS

The US National Weather Service needs help to spot twisters ahead of time. Many areas of Tornado Alley have networks of specially trained people who swing into action during a tornado watch. This group of storm spotters is called the SKYWARN Network.

Storm spotters who see a tornado alert the Weather Service so that it can issue a tornado warning. Their sharp eyes and training have saved many lives.

FEMA agents surveyed tornado damage in Lexington, Kentucky, USA, after a twister tore through the town in 2004.

When a disaster strikes a poor region, people there may not have enough resources to recover. That's when help from the outside is so important. Other countries and private relief organizations may send disaster relief teams and supplies. The International Red Cross and Red Crescent Movement is also a major source of aid.

People also donate money or volunteer to help tornado victims. In 1880 W D Chitty remembered that 'the whole world seemed to respond in sympathy and practical generosity to stricken little Marshfield.'

At first, relief workers may start by providing emergency medical help to injured people. They may also help rescue workers find people trapped in the wreckage of buildings. Later, they often help people set up shelters in schools and other big buildings. Tornado disaster victims whose homes have been damaged or destroyed can stay at these shelters for a few days.

HOW CAN YOU HELP?

One of the best ways to help people affected by a disaster is to donate money to an organization that is helping the victims. Money allows those organizations to buy exactly what they need. The British Red Cross (www.redcross.org.uk) often is among the first organizations to arrive at a disaster scene.

GETTING A LIFE BACK

Victims of tornadoes and other disasters often need money to get their lives back to normal. This is especially important when a tornado destroys much of a town, as the 1974 twister in Xenia, Ohio, did. When businesses, factories and farms are destroyed, many people are left with no place to work. This makes it hard for them to earn money until the damage is repaired.

'Where we ever got the money to rebuild so promptly has always been a mystery,' Chitty said about Marshfield. 'But the fact is that little time was lost in restoring the town to its former business capacity.'

The people of Xenia also rebuilt their town. They got help from the US government, through special loans to disaster victims. Starting over is not easy, but most communities damaged by tornadoes do rebuild eventually. People do get a life back again.

Canine (dog) search crews gather outside a collapsed
building in Pierce City, Missouri, USA, where citizens
had been seeking shelter from violent storms. The dogs
helped search for survivors of a series of tornadoes
that had swept through the town in 2003.

A woman weeps after a tornado levelled her home in Bangladesh in 1996.

1996
DISASTER IN BANGLADESH

In 1996 Babul Ahmed was ten years old. He and his family lived in Rampur, a village in Bangladesh. This South Asian country is near India. On the evening of 13 May Babul's family knew a storm was brewing when the wind started blowing and rain poured down. But they didn't expect a tornado.

With winds whirling up to 200 kmph, the tornado tore buildings apart as if they were built from sand. *'It was dust and wind everywhere,'* said Babul. The winds picked up people, farm animals and carts as if they were feathers. About 55 of Babul's neighbours died. Hundreds more were injured. *'We heard cries for help from everywhere but could see nothing,'* said one man.

Relatives surround the bodies of loved ones, victims of the 1996 twister that killed more than 600 people and injured more than 30,000 others.

The **whole village** *has diminished into a* **vast grave.**

– a police officer in the village of Barabhita, not far from Rampur

As the twister came roaring towards another village, people ran into the police station. Bangladesh is a poor country, where many families live crowded together in small houses. These homes are often poorly built out of rickety materials. They would fall apart easily in the tornado's winds. The police station was the strongest building in the village. People thought they would be safe there, but the tornado's winds were too strong even for this building. In all, more than 100 people died in that village.

The tornado continued to rip through central Bangladesh, striking 80 villages other than Babul's. In the whole disaster zone, more than 600 people were killed and tens of thousands were injured. Local hospitals were soon overflowing with patients. They ran out of medicine, bandages and other supplies. Some injured people waited hours or days for a doctor or nurse. Others died because there were not enough emergency workers to help.

The tornado completely destroyed at least 10,000 houses, damaging thousands of others. More than 100,000 people were left homeless. The storm also snapped telephone lines and uprooted trees. It destroyed farmers' crops and killed cows and other farm animals. Even after the tornado passed, it took days for help to arrive. When it did, residents of the ruined towns began to rebuild their lives, but they would never be the same again

45

The Future

'ATTENTION! A TORNADO WILL FORM NEAR SMITHBURG BETWEEN NINE AND ELEVEN O'CLOCK TONIGHT. BY MIDNIGHT IT WILL MOVE DOWN MAIN STREET. THEN IT WILL GO DOWN HIGHWAY 86 TOWARDS THE NEW TOWN SHOPPING CENTRE. EVERYONE IN THOSE AREAS SHOULD LEAVE OR TAKE COVER.'

Weather forecasters in the United States wish they could give people that kind of advance warning about tornadoes. They could save many lives if they could tell, hours ahead of time, whether a tornado will form, when it will hit, and where it will go. The more advance warning people have, the better they can prepare for a disaster. Unfortunately, this kind of detailed information is still in the future.

In the past, people had little or no warning. Sometimes they just looked out the window and saw a tornado approaching. Other times, they heard a roar like a train and suddenly found that a tornado was right in their back garden. Even with modern technology, warnings do not always come in time. 'I heard something and I thought it was hail,' said Chuck Smith, who was at work in Stoneville, North Carolina, USA, in 1998 when a twister hit without warning. 'Then, two seconds later, the roof started lifting off.'

A Doppler radar station in Norman, Oklahoma, USA.

By studying past storms, scientists and weather forecasters have learned a lot about what might happen in future tornadoes. They know, for example, the weather conditions that can produce tornadoes. In the UK the Met Office works hard to predict accurate storm and tornado warnings.

'*Your mind could not accept what you were seeing. It couldn't be – but it was.*'

– Lisa Irene Hale, recalling the 1974 Super Outbreak

{ A tornado approaching an Oklahoma City house in July 1980.

WATCHES AND WARNINGS

People learn about severe weather alerts from television, radio and the Internet. In the US there are two kinds of tornado alerts – watches and warnings. A tornado watch means that weather conditions are right for a tornado. It tells people to stay tuned to their radio for further information. Watches usually last two to six hours and cover an area of thousands of square kilometres.

A tornado warning means that a tornado has actually been spotted. It tells people to take cover immediately. Some cities turn on a special warning siren to make sure everyone knows about the danger. Most tornado warnings cover small areas, such as a county or city and usually last less than an hour.

This military aeroplane was damaged in a 1948 tornado that swept through Tinker Air Force Base in Oklahoma, USA. The first broadcast tornado warning occurred during this storm.

BETTER TORNADO TECHNOLOGY

After the devastating 1974 Tornado Super Outbreak the US National Weather Service realized that it needed better technology to detect tornadoes. The Weather Service spent about $4.5 billion to modernize weather forecasting technology.

'What we saw [in 1974] as a green blob on [an old] radar scope is now depicted in full colour and high resolution detail,' said John Forsing. He helped forecast the Super Outbreak for the Weather Service. 'With modernized technology such as Doppler radar, weather satellites and advanced computers, forecasters can now pinpoint tornadoes even before they touch down.'

This radar screen shows a hook echo, a type of storm formation that often leads to tornadoes.

With help from these new tools, the National Weather Service in the US issues about 15,000 severe storm and tornado watches and warnings each year. New technology and better scientific knowledge allow forecasters to issue those warnings sooner. People usually have about twelve minutes' advance notice of severe weather. This is twice as much time as they had as recently as the mid-1990s. People also get more accurate alerts than they used to. In 1974 forecasts were only half as accurate as they are in the early twenty-first century.

Computers help weather forecasters tell when severe storms will happen. In the future, more powerful computers will probably produce even better forecasts. They will give individuals and communities more time to prepare for tornadoes. This extra time is very important. It helps save lives and can also reduce the amount of property damage.

BEING PREPARED

Have you ever heard the expression 'forewarned is forearmed'? It means that if you know what's about to happen you can prepare yourself for it. People in the United States who live in areas that often suffer from tornadoes have to be well-prepared. Some families in Tornado Alley have built underground tornado shelters

These students are practising tornado safety – crouching against a solid, interior wall and protecting their heads. Most schools in the USA perform such drills to prepare students in the event of a real disaster.

Ten neighbours in Moore, Oklahoma, USA, were trapped for more than an hour in this storm shelter. A 2003 tornado had swept through the town, blocking the shelter's exit with debris.

or safe rooms. These specially built places can withstand winds of up to 402 kmph and 160 kmph hits by flying debris. They survive even if their house is flattened. Other Americans dash into their cellars. This underground room is the safest place in the house. Staying away from windows and hiding under a piece of sturdy furniture or a mattress is another way for them to protect themselves. Many tornadoes strike when people are asleep and not listening to television or radio warnings. A community tornado siren can wake up sleeping people and save lives. Sirens and shelters can be especially important in mobile home communities, where tornadoes often cause great damage. Mobile homes should be anchored securely to the ground. People living in mobile home parks should know about separate shelters in their communities. These shelters are built specifically to keep people safe during tornadoes and other emergencies.

TORNADO MYTHS & FACTS

MYTH: Open windows in your house, or it will explode as the vacuum inside a tornado sucks up air outside.
FACT: Don't waste the time. Instead, head for shelter. The wind and debris from a tornado will probably break the windows.

MYTH: The south-west corner of your cellar is the safest place during a tornado.
FACT: Tornadoes often come from the south-west, so that maybe the most dangerous place to hide. The very safest place is a cellar room with no windows and sturdy walls.

MYTH: Tornadoes never strike big cities.
FACT: Tornadoes are relatively rare in big cities, but nowhere has natural protection from a tornado. Twisters have hit several large US cities, such as Oklahoma City, Oklahoma; Miami, Florida; Fort Worth, Texas; Nashville, Tennessee; and Salt Lake City, Utah.

A September 2005 tornado in Minnesota, USA,
tore part of the roof off this couple's home. In
the Mid-west, it is extremely rare to
experience tornadoes so late in the season.

New construction methods are being used to build stronger homes and other buildings. For example, special tornado clips keep roofs attached to buildings when a tornado tries to suck them up. Better ways of attaching mobile homes to the ground are important too.

Tornadoes are frightening, and they can cause terrible disasters. Being prepared, however, is much better than being scared. The more information people have about tornadoes, the better they will understand the threat – and the better able they will be to protect themselves if a twister ever hits.

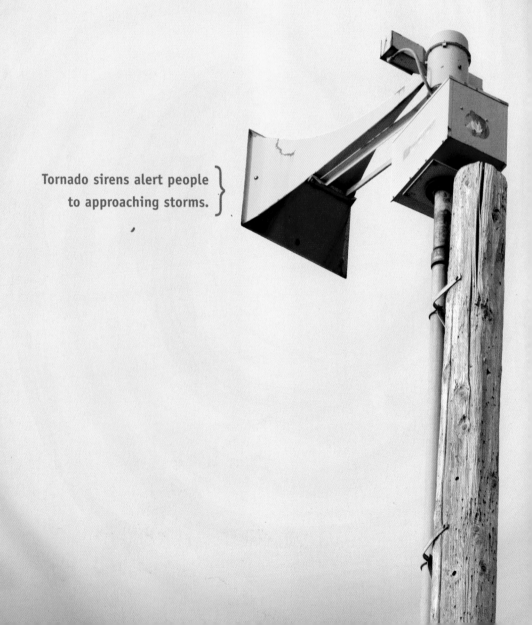

Tornado sirens alert people to approaching storms.

TORNADO SAFETY RULES

You and your family can stay safe during a tornado emergency by following a few simple rules.

DURING A TORNADO WATCH:

- Listen to local radio and television stations for updates.

- Watch the weather nearby. Strong winds or a roaring sound like a freight train may mean a tornado is approaching.

DURING A TORNADO WARNING:

- If you are inside, go to the safe place that you and your family picked in advance to protect yourself from glass and other flying objects.

- If you are outside, lie flat in a ditch or low-lying area, or hurry to the cellar of the closest sturdy building.

- If you are in a car or mobile home, get out. Head for one of the safe places above.

AFTER A TORNADO PASSES:

- Watch for fallen electric power lines. Do not touch any that you find.

- Stay out of the damaged area.

- Listen to the radio for information and instructions.

- Do not light matches or candles. They could cause explosions or fires if gas is leaking into the air.

Timeline

1840 The Great Natchez Tornado strikes Mississippi, USA, killing at least 317 people.

1880 A tornado, spotted by W D Chitty, destroys much of Marshfield, Missouri.

1882 A tornado in Iowa, USA, kills more than 100 people.

1884 About 800 people are killed by a series of 60 tornadoes sweeping through the south-eastern United States *(below, right)*.

1889 A single tornado is responsible for the deaths of 119 citizens in New Richmond, Wisconsin, USA.

1896 Approximately 300 citizens of Saint Louis, Missouri, USA, are killed by a powerful twister.

1925 The Tri-State Tornado, the deadliest tornado in US history, strikes Missouri, Illinois and Indiana, killing nearly 700 people.

1936 Several twisters race through the southern United States in early April. One strikes Gainesville, Georgia *(left)*, killing more than 100 people. Gainesville had already been hit in 1903 and would be hit again in 1944.

1948 The first tornado forecast is made. Forecasting leads to tornado observation and prediction centres, saving thousands of lives each year.

1951 Theodore Fujita invents a scale to measure the intensity of tornadoes.

1953 A tornado hits Flint in the state of Michigan, USA, *(facing page, top)*. It kills more than 100 people and demolishes hundreds of homes. The storm moves eastwards and forms another tornado in Massachusetts. This twister kills dozens, covers 75 km (45 miles) and spends 90 minutes on the ground. Debris is swept eastward into Massachusetts Bay and the Atlantic Ocean.

1965 More than 36 tornadoes strike the mid-western United States, killing more than 250 people.

1969 A twister in Dakha, Bangladesh (then East Pakistan), kills 540 people and leaves 80,000 homeless.

1973 A tornado hits San Justo, Argentina, killing 54 and injuring 500 others.

1974 The Super Tornado Outbreak sweeps across the Mid-west.

1979 The Wichita Falls, Texas, USA tornado causes $400 million of damage. An early warning system saves most citizens.

1985 On 31 May, a series of 41 tornadoes strikes the north-eastern United States, causing 90 deaths.

1990 A tornado destroys most of Limon, Colorado, causing $12 million of damage.

1991 An outbreak of more than 50 tornadoes strikes six states in the Mid-west.

1995 A small but powerful tornado in Pampa, Texas, USA, causes $30 million of damage *(right)*.

1996 A tornado in Bangladesh kills more than 600 people.

1999 In one day, 59 tornadoes touch down in central Oklahoma, USA.

1999 In South Africa, the Mount Ayliff tornado kills 25 people and injures 500 others.

2003 During a single week in early May, approximately 400 tornadoes strike the United States.

2005 Tornado hits Birmingham in Britain, injuring 19 people and damaging over 100 houses.

2006 In the USA at least 50 tornadoes sweep through 8 states in the Mid-west and South, killing at least 27 people.

2006 The Kensal Rise area of London is hit by a tornado. Cars and houses are badly damaged.

Glossary

debris: pieces of buildings or other things that have been destroyed. Tornadoes pick up debris such as bricks, wooden beams and broken glass.

Doppler radar: a special kind of radar that shows and measures wind directions and speeds. Doppler readings help scientists and weather forecasters learn about the formation and movement of tornadoes.

mesocyclone: spinning air inside a supercell. Some mesocyclones produce tornadoes.

meteorologist: a scientist who studies the weather

supercell: a severe thunderstorm with strong winds

tornado warning: a weather alert when a tornado has been spotted in the area or has shown up on local radar. During a warning, people should take cover.

tornado watch: a weather alert given when conditions in a region are right for producing tornadoes. During a watch, a tornado has not yet been spotted.

updraught: a rising current of air

wall cloud: a spinning cloud formation that hangs down from a supercell and looks like a dark wall of clouds hanging in the sky. Some wall clouds produce tornadoes.

waterspout: a funnel cloud that forms over a body of water

weather front: the boundary where two masses of air with different conditions meet

wind shear: a change or difference in wind speed, direction, or both. In a supercell, wind shear can create a wide, horizontal tube of rapidly spinning air.

Places to Visit

The Sciene Museum London
http://www.sciencemuseum.org.uk
The Science Museum in London has an exciting exhibition on weather. The Weather Gallery explores the science of weather and tells the story of how scientists from the 1700s to the present day have measured and recorded rainfall, air pressure, wind speed, temperature, humidity and hours of sunshine.

Source Notes

4   Cable News Network, 'Tornado Kills 22 in Indiana', *CNN.com*, 7 November 2005, http://www.cnn.com/2005/WEATHER/11/06/indiana.tornadoes/ (10 January 2006).

4   WorldNow and WFIE, 'Historic Tornado Outbreak Sunday,' *WFIE*, 6 November 2005, http://www.14wfie.com/Global/story.asp?S=4077888 (10 January 2006).

4   Ibid.

4   CNN, 'Tornado Kills 22 in Indiana'.

4   Reuters, '23 Dead in US Tornado Destruction,' *ABC News Online*, 8 November 2005, http://www.abc.net.au/news/newsitems/200511/s1499955.htm (31 January 2006).

5   Cable News Network, 'The Whole House Just Exploded,' *CNN.com*, 8 November 2005, http://www.cnn.com/2005/WEATHER/11/07/tornado/ (10 January 2006).

6   Mark Scolforo, 'Tornado Survivors Recount Harrowing Tales,' *phillyBurbs.com*, 15 July 2004, http://www.phillyburbs.com/pb-dyn/news/103-07152004-331825.html (17 October 2005).

8   Homer G Ramby, 'Don E Halsey– Meteorologists,' *Xenia Tornado*, n.d., http://www.xeniatornado.com/vwso.htm (17 October 2005).

9   Scott Koerner, 'Survivor Stories from Brandenburg,' *Tornado Super Outbreak–April 3, 1974*, n.d., http://www.april31974.com/survivor_stories_from_brandenburg.htm (17 October 2005).

10 UAW Local 2209, 'Oklahoma City GM Plant Tornado Damage', *UAW Local 2209*, 9 May 2003, http://www.local2209.org/default100b.asp (17 October 2005).

10 'Marshfield Missouri–Tornado', *Sho-Me Power Electric Cooperative*, n.d., http://www.shomepower.com/tornado.htm (17 October 2005).

12–13   Ibid.

13 Ibid.

14 NOAA, 'Cold Front Spawns Super-Cell Storms, Deadly Tornadoes in Central Plains States', *NOAA News Online*, 5 May 2003, http://www.noaanews.noaa.gov/stories/s1136.htm (17 October 2005).

22 NOAA, 'Interesting Quotes', 1925 *Tri-State Tornado: A Look Back*, 2005, http://www.crh.noaa.gov/pah/1925/iq_body.html (October 17, 2005).

22–23   Ibid.

23 Ibid.

23 Lee Davis, *Natural Disasters*, New York: Facts on File, 2002, 314.

23 NOAA, 'Interesting Quotes',

23 Ibid.

28 Homer G Ramby, 'Rick Hoag', *Xenia Tornado*, n.d., http://www.xeniatornado.com/hoag.htm (17 October 2005).

29 Ibid.

30 Scott Koerner, 'Survivor Stories from Brandenburg'.

31 WorldNow and WOODTV, '1956: Michigan's Most Destructive Tornado', *WOODTV.com*, n.d., http://www.woodtv.com/Global/story.asp?S=759210 (10 January 2006).

36 Justin L and Niki M, 'Survivors' Stories', *Twisters: Destruction from the Sky*, n.d., http://library.thinkquest.org/4232/survivor.htm (17 October 2005).

37 NOAA, 'Interesting Quotes'.

37 Justin L and Niki M, 'Survivors' Stories.'

38 Homer G Ramby, 'Lisa Irene (Pagett) Hale', *Xenia Tornado*, n.d., http://www.xeniatornado.com/hale.htm (17 October 2005).

40 Jim Brocker and Conni James, 'An Eyewitness Account of the Tornado's Devastation', *Gazette.net*, 1 May 2002, http://gazette.net/gazette_archive/2002/200218/montgomerycty/state/102300-1.html (17 October 2005).

40 'Marshfield Missouri', *Sho-Me Power*.

42 Ibid.

42 Ibid.

44 Cable News Network, 'Aid Rushed to Bangladesh Tornado Victims', *CNN.com*, 15 May 1996, http://www.cnn.com/WORLD/9605/15/bangladesh (17 October 2005).

44 Cable News Network, 'Tornado Kills More Than 400 in Bangladesh', *CNN.com*, 14 May 1996, http://www.cnn.com/WORLD/9605/14/bangladesh/index.html (17 October 2005).

45 Ibid.

46 Taft Wireback, 'Survivors Tell Their Tornado Tales', *News & Record Online*, March 21, 1998, http://www.news-record.com/news/indepth/tornado/survivor.shtml (10 January 2006).

47 Homer G. Ramby, 'Lisa Irene (Pagett) Hale.'

48 National Oceanic and Atmospheric Administration, 'Weather Service Commemorates Nation's Worst Tornado Outbreak', *NOAA and the 1974 Tornado Outbreak*, n.d., http://www.publicaffairs.noaa.gov/storms/release.html (17 October 2005).

Selected Bibliography

Akin, Wallace E. *The Forgotten Storm: The Great Tri-State Tornado of 1925*. Guilford, CT: Lyons Press, 2002.

Allaby, Michael. *A Chronology of Weather: Dangerous Weather*. New York: Facts on File, Inc., 1998.

Bedard, Richard. *In The Shadow of the Tornado: Stories and Adventures from the Heart of Storm Country*. Norman, OK: Gilco Publishing, 1996.

Bradford, Marlene. *Scanning the Skies: A History of Tornado Forecasting*. Norman: University of Oklahoma Press, 2001.

Capella, Chris. 'Tornadoes Are Earth's Most Violent Storms.' *USATODAY.com*. 17 May 2005. http://www.usatoday.com/weather/resources/basics/twist0.htm (17October 2005).

Centers for Disease Control and Prevention. 'Tornadoes.' *Emergency Preparedness and Response: Natural Disasters and Severe Weather*. 2003. http://www.bt.cdc.gov/disasters/tornadoes/index.asp (12 October 2005).

Davidson, Keay. *Twister: The Science of Tornadoes and the Making of an Adventure Movie*. New York: Pocket Books, 1996.

Davis, Lee. *Natural Disasters*. New York: Facts on File, 2002.

Edwards, Roger. 'The Online Tornado FAQ.' *NOAA's National Weather Service: Storm Prediction Center*. N.d. http://www.spc.noaa.gov/faq/tornado/index.html (12 October 2005).

Hancock, Paul L., and Brian J. Skinner, eds. *The Oxford Companion to the Earth*. New York: Oxford University Press, 2000.

Hemingway, Lorian. *A World Turned Over: A Killer Tornado and the Lives It Changed Forever*. New York: Simon & Schuster, 2002.

National Oceanic and Atmospheric Administration. 'Eyewitness Account: Bobby Boyd.' *NOAA and the 1974 Tornado Outbreak*. N.d. http://www.publicaffairs.noaa.gov/storms/boyd.html (12 October 2005).

——. *Thunderstorms . . . Tornadoes . . . Lightning: Nature's Most Violent Storms*. N.d. http://www.nws.noaa.gov/om/brochures/ttl.pdf (12 October 2005).

Newson, Lesley. *Devastation! The World's Worst Natural Disasters*. New York: Dorling Kindersley Publishing, 1998.

Pearson Education. 'U.S. Tornadoes.' *Infoplease*. N.d. http://infoplease.com/ipa/A0001445.html (12 October 2005).

Robinson, Andrew. *Earth Shock: Hurricanes, Volcanoes, Earthquakes, Tornadoes and Other Forces of Nature*. London: Thames & Hudson, 2002.

Rosenfeld, Jeffrey. *Eye of the Storm: Inside the World's Deadliest Hurricanes, Tornadoes and Blizzards*. New York: Plenum Trade, 1999.

University of Wisconsin Board of Regents. 'Tornado Disaster: 39 Dead.' *Twister: The Tornado Story*. 2003. http://whyfiles.org/013tornado/2.html (12 October 2005).

Ward. Kaari, ed. *Great Disasters: Dramatic True Stories of Nature's Awesome Powers*. Pleasantville, NY: Reader's Digest Association, 1989.

Further Resources

BOOKS

Baldwin, Carol. *Storm Warning: Tornadoes* (Turbulent Planet). Raintree Publishers, 2004.

Baldwin, Carol. *Violent Skies - Hurricanes* (Turbulent Planet) Raintree Publishers, 2005.

Baum, L Frank. *The Wonderful Wizard of Oz* Oxford Paperbacks, 2000.

Challoner, Jack. *Hurricane and Tornado* (Eyewitness Books). Dorling Kindersley Publishing, 2000.

Chambers, Catherine. *Tornado* (Wild Weather) Heinemann Library, 2008.

Collins, Andrew. *Violent Weather: Thunderstorms, Tornadoes, and Hurricanes* (National Geographic Science Chapters) National Geographic Society, 2006.

Connolly, Sean. *Storms* (In Time of Need). Franklin Watts Ltd, 2004.

Langley, Andrew. *Natural Disasters* (Kingfisher Knowledge) Kingfisher Books Ltd, 2006.

Morris, Neil. *Hurricanes and Tornadoes* (Snapping-Turtle Guides). Ticktock Media Ltd, 2004.

Oxlade, Chris. *Storm Warning-Tornadoes* (Turbulent Planet) Raintree Publishers, 2005.

Pipe, Jim. Weather and Climate (Planet Earth) Ticktock Media Ltd, 2008.

Spilsbury, Louise and Richard Spilsbury. *Terrifying Tornadoes* (Awesome Forces of Nature). Heinemann Library, 2004.

Steele, Chris. *Tornadoes* (Nature on the Rampage). Raintree, 2004.

Violent Planet (Phenomena). Ticktock Media Ltd, 2006.

Watts, Claire. *Natural Disasters: Discover the Awesome Power of Tsunamis, Hurricanes, Earthquakes and Volcanoes* (Eyewitness Guide) Dorling Kindersley Publishers Ltd, 2006.

Watts, Claire. *Natural Disasters* (DK Eyewitness Books) DK Publishing, 2006.

Waters, Fiona. *Storms* (Our Violent Earth). Hodder Wayland, 2001.

Weather (Eyewitness Guide) Dorling Kindersley Publishers Ltd, 2007.

WEBSITES AND FILMS

BBC Weather
http://www.bbc.co.uk/weather/weatherwise/fact-files/extremes/tornadoes.shtml
This website has detailed information on how tornadoes are formed

The Met Office
http://www.metoffice.gov.uk/education/second-ary/students/tornadoes.html
The UK met office site has loads of facts on how, when and why tornadoes occur. It also looks at how tornadoes can be predicted and how the damage they cause is measured

National Geographic: Eye in the Sky – Tornadoes
http://www.nationalgeographic.com/eye/tornadoes/tornadoes.html
The 'Eye in the Sky' shows a twister and its after-math in graphic detail.

Sky Diary KIDSTORM
http://skydiary.com/kids
Find facts about violent storms including torna-does and hurricanes.

SKYWARN National Home Page
http://www.skywarn.org
Visit this site, from an organization of storm spot-ters and chasers, to see many maps of U.S. weather conditions. The SKYWARN Network helps alert local emergency management agencies about possible twisters and other threats.

Tornadoes – Dan's Wild Weather Page
http://www.wildwildweather.com/twisters.htm
Find answers to many questions about tornadoes at this site. Be sure to visit the Fujita scale page at http://www.wildwildweather.com/fujita.htm.

Tornado Project Online
http://www.tornadoproject.com
This website presents a wealth of tornado infor-mation, from myths to safety tips.

Forces of Nature. Directed by George Casey. Washington, DC: National Geographic Society, 2004. DVD.
This thrilling film shows the overwhelming power of tornadoes and documents the damage they cause.

Nature's Fury. Directed by Jaime Bernank: National Geographic Society, 1994. DVD.
Join tornado hunters on the job, and learn the methods they use to predict where these destruc-tive storms will strike.

Twister. Directed by Jan de Bont: UCA Catalogue, 2006.
This action film tells the story of a two thrill-seeking meteorologists who chase tornadoes in order to study them.

The Wizard of Oz. Directed by Victor Fleming. Hollywood, CA: Warner Bros. Studios, 1939. DVD.
This is the classic film of Dorothy, Toto, the Tin Man, the Scarecrow and the Cowardly Lion, who find themselves together after a tornado carries Dorothy from Kansas to Oz.

Index

Photo Acknowledegments

The photographs in this book are used with the permission of: Marvin Nauman/FEMA, p 1; Courtesy of the National Oceanic and Atmospheric Administration Central Library Photo Collection, pp 3, 16, 17, 19, 21, 23 (both), 24 (both), 25, 29 (top), 34, 36, 37 (both), 46, 48, 49, 55, 56 (top); © Reuters/CORBIS, pp 4, 38, 43; © John Sommers II/Reuters/CORBIS, p 5; © Holger Otto/Reuters/CORBIS, p 7; © Everett Collection, p 8 (top); © Bettmann/CORBIS, pp 8 (bottom), 9, 22, 29 (bottom), 31, 32, 35, 56 (bottom); © Eric Nguyen/Jim Reed Photography/CORBIS, p 11; Webster County Historical Society, pp 12, 13 (top); State Historical Society of Missouri, Columbia, p 13 (bottom); © Jim Reed/CORBIS, p 14; © Zhangjian-Jiangsu/ImageChina/ZUMA Press, p 15; © iStockphoto.com, p 18; © Andrew Fox/CORBIS, 20; © Michael Mauney/Time Life Pictures/Getty Images, p 28; © James Gibbard/Tulsa World/ZUMA Press, p 33; © David Crenshaw/Tulsa World/ZUMA Press, pp 39, 51; Michael Rieger/FEMA, p 41; © Farjana K Godhuly/AFP/Getty Images, p 44; © AP Photo/Pavel Rahman, p 45; © NOAA/ZUMA Press, p 47; © Todd Strand/Independent Picture Service, p 50; © Stormi Greener/Minneapolis Star Tribune/ZUMA Press, p 53; © Sam Lund/Independent Picture Service, p 54; © John G Zimmerman/Time Life Pictures/Getty Images, p 57 (top); © Harald Richter/AFP/Getty Images, p 57 (middle); © Joseph C Garza/US Navy/Handout/Reuters/CORBIS, p 57 (bottom). Diagram by © Bill Hauser/Independent Picture Service, p 21.

Front Cover: © Jim Zuckerman/CORBIS; Back Cover: Courtesy of the National Oceanic and Atmospheric Administration Central Library Photo Collection.

About the Authors

Michael Woods is a science and medical journalist in Washington, DC, who has won many national writing awards. He works in the Washington Bureau of the *Pittsburgh Post-Gazette* and the *Toledo Blade*. Mary B Woods has been a librarian in the Fairfax County Public School System in Virginia, USA, and the Benjamin Franklin International School in Barcelona, Spain. Their other books include the eight-volume Ancient Technology series. Michael and Mary have four children. When not writing, reading or enjoying their grandchildren, they travel to gather material for future books.